EARLY HISTORY OF AUSTRALIA

As so often in history, the greatest achievements happen by accident. The discovery of Australia by Europeans happened the same way.

It was the Dutch explorer Dirk Hartog, who while capitalising on those trade winds — the roaring forties — was caught in a gale which lasted for three days. Driven further east than Hartog could ever envisage, he unwittingly stumbled on an island just off the west coast of Australia (now Dirk Hartog Island). He immediately knew that this must be the Great South Land. A plate on a post was erected on which he engraved:

DIRK HARTOG WAS HERE ON 25TH OF OCTOBER 1616
WITH HIS SHIP THE EENDRACHT.

In 1642, the Governor General of Batavia, (now Djakarta) Anthony Van Diemen, gave orders to thoroughly investigate the coast of New Holland. He wanted an exact map of the entire continent, hoping to find another promising South Land.

It was Abel Tasman, a man who, after serving ten years with the Dutch East India Company, was chosen to undertake the historic journey. In 1644 he returned with a sensational map. He had discovered what is now Tasmania, and named it Van Diemen's Land, to honour his employer.

For the next 130 years Tasman's map remained valid. Even Captain James Cook in 1769 used this map to fulfill his task.

When Cook found the east coast of the Great South Land, he not only hoisted the British Flag on what is now Botany Bay, he also brought back to England an entire map of the east coast which he had named New South Wales. When he gave the name Port Jackson to a harbour, (which he never saw) and after the first settlers arrived in 1788, who would have believed that this would become the place for Australia's most beautiful city on the harbour — Sydney.

Although 200 years have past and Australia has become a continent of different states, tourists and locals alike are still discovering the enchanting beauty of what was once called the Great South Land.

The rugged, but beautiful coastline of the Great Ocean Road in Victoria. Millions of years of erosion and heavy pounding of the sea formed this impressive Archway.

SYDNEY

Sydney, with some 3.5 million people is the glamour city of Australia.

Situated around the finest harbour in the World, life never stops. From early morning majestic cruise ships float past the Opera House and million dollar mansions. At night the brilliant lights of Sydney reflect in the harbour giving an unforgetable impression.

Where the night life is as intoxicating as a bottle of champagne, Kings Cross is the place to spend your last energy until the early morning hours.

Surrounded by National Parks and mighty rivers, Sydney has some 37 beaches, an asset no other city in the world can claim.

Aerial view over Sydney's magnificent harbour.

The Rocks.

Darling Harbour.

The Three Sisters.

THE BLUE MOUNTAINS

The Blue Mountains, part of the Great Dividing Range, which run parallel to the east coast of Australia for more than 4,000 km, are a natural wonder.

Unlike anywhere else in the world, the deep blue hue, which gave the Mountains there name, is caused by the scattering of light as it comes into contact with dust and droplets of oil emitted by the leaves of the eucalyptus trees.

A tourist mecca, just 65 km west of Sydney, the Blue Mountains offer spectacular cable car rides 300 metres above Jamieson Valley, or a plunge 250 metres down onto the world's steepest railway. The most famous landmarks are that of the triple rock pillars known as the Three Sisters, and the Jenolan Caves.

Jenolan Caves.

The Great Hawkesbury River.

Springtime in the Warrumbungle National Park, near Coonabarabran N.S.W.

Cape Byron, Australia's most easterly point.

Minyon Falls near Lismore.
A spectacular waterfall surrounded by lush rainforest in northern New South Wales.

CANBERRA

Australia's Capital has certainly come a long way since Walter Burley Griffin's vision first began to take shape along the shores of the lake now named after him.

Canberra is now a bustling city and one of Australia's most popular tourist destinations. Not only is it the seat of Parliament, it also boasts some of the most spectacular public buildings, parks and gardens.

Looking down Anzac Parade towards Australia's Parliament House.

Telecom Tower, Black Mountain.

View over Lake Burley Griffin from Black Mountain.

Downhill skiing — most popular.

THE SNOWY MOUNTAINS

The mighty Snowy Mountains — Australia's highest — offer incomparable skiing, mountaineering and a summer paradise of alpine wildflowers.

Frozen landscape.

A winter wonderland.

MELBOURNE

Capital of the Garden State, Melbourne provides sweeping green lawns, tree lined boulevards and gardens ablaze with colour throughout the year. Majestic buildings from the days of Queen Victoria provide Melbourne with a special old world charm.

Government foresight decreed that Melbourne was to have plenty of open spaces and today wide thoroughfares allow Melbourne to boast the only public tram system existing in Australia.

Bourke Street Mall.

Evening lights of Melbourne Skyline

The bustling Bourke Street.

The Victorian Arts Centre.

Peace and tranquillity in the Grampians.

The Grampians Victoria.

AUSTRALIA'S BUSHLAND

The real essence of Australia can only be found in the bush.

The wild, natural beauty of this great land, born in the dawn of time, remains largely unspoilt for us to enjoy today.

Sheep grazing.

Like chess pieces waiting for the next move, the intriguing Twelve Apostles sit dormant.

The Arch.

The London Bridge before millions of years of erosion forced its collapse.

View over Australia's first casino — the Wrest Point Federal Hotel-Casino, Hobart.

TASMANIA

Tasmania is an enchanting island of contrasts, a land of lush green countryside, rustic colonial villages, majestic mountains, beautiful wilderness and rugged coastlines.

Evidence of Tasmania's historic past and old world charm matches the mood of this tranquil island paradise.

The Quadrant Mall, Launceston.

The old church — Port Arthur's most beautiful building.

The magic Gordon River.

ADELAIDE

City of Churches, on the banks of the Torrens River, Adelaide, is home to the internationally acclaimed Festival of Arts. Held every second March, the Adelaide Festival lights up the city with talent and excitement.

For those who appreciate the fast life, every year for one week decorum is lost when the Formula One Grand Prix revs out a 3.78 km course through Adelaide's peaceful streets.

More relaxed, the picturesque vineyards of the Barossa Valley, McLaren Vale and Clare Valley provide their own special blend of hospitality and charm.

St. Peters Cathedral.

Picturesque Adelaide by night.

Victoria Square.

View across the Torrens River.

Cobweb silhouetted against the morning sun.

South Australia is the acknowledged wine state of Australia, particularly Barossa Valley, Clare Valley and McLaren Vale.

Each year as October turns to November, the week long McLaren Vale Wine Bushing Festival offers wine tasting, informative tours and, as a grand finale, an Elizabethan Feast.

Succulent red grapes.

Homestead nestled against the imposing Flinders Ranges.

The Flinders Ranges begin some 250 kilometres north of Adelaide near Peterborough, but the most beautiful valleys and peaks are northeast of Port Augusta. The Flinders also have a variety of vegetation and trees, such as River Red Gums, Wattles, Casuarinas and Pine.

A colourful array of beautiful Australian wildflowers.

The Pinnacle Desert. Limestone pillars rising from the sand dunes of the Nambung National Park, create an eerie atmosphere.

The awe-inspiring cliffs of Australia's rugged coastline.

Typical road signs found in the outback.

Outback windmills.

Sturt's Desert Pea.

Perth glows during the day and night.

The superb "Swans" fountain guarding the Burswood Casino.

PERTH

Perth, the relaxed capital with unpolluted blue skies has an atmosphere of its own.

Built around the picturesque Swan River and bordered by the beaches of an endless ocean, Perth offers extreme beauty. It simply has more of everything — more space, more sunshine, more wildflowers and more astonishing contrasts than you'll see on most continents.

Historic Fremantle, famous for the America's Cup Challenge, provides a brooding old world atmosphere of solid Victorian buildings with a pub on each corner.

Prolific and brilliant wildflowers are the West's greatest delight. A brilliant kaleidoscope of colour from an enormous range of flowers, famous the world over, are plentiful throughout the State.

The picturesque London Court.

The ever popular Fremantle markets.

The gigantic Karri Trees, growing to a height of 60 metres and more.

Albany, just over 400 kilometres south of Perth is a very beautiful part of the south coast and is the principle port at the southern tip of Western Australia.

Wave Rock.

Wave rock is situated 350 kilometres east of Perth near Hyden. The rock is similar to other granites that occur throughout this part of Western Australia.

Scientific studies have revealed that they are 2,700 million years old. Wave rock has been formed by weathering processes and erosion which over long periods of time have created the undercut surface of the rock.

The pronounced vertical bands of colour have been formed by rain washing chemical deposits down the slope.

Kalgoorlie.

MINING — In the beginning of the 1890's the gold rush shifted to Western Australia. Gold was found in Coolgardie in 1892, but the big rush started one year later in Kalgoorlie, becoming the biggest gold producing town in Australia up to the present time.

Goldmine.

The Backyards.

Coolgardie — The first National Bank.

Have a beer at Coolgardie.

Aerial view of Coober Pedy.

Lightning Ridge N.S.W., home of the Black Opal. Unlike open cut mining, digging underground still holds a certain fascination of finding the "Big One".

Dust storm about to engulf the tiny outback town of Urandangi as viewed from the Federal Hotel. The Dangi Pub is a popular stopover for travellers taking the more adventurous "tourist route" between Mt. Isa and Alice Springs.

BRISBANE

Host to World Expo 88, the International highlight of Australia's Bicentenary, is Brisbane, Queensland's capital.

Brisbane is a rambling city of green semi-tropical outdoor living. On the shores of the meandering Brisbane River, brilliant sunshine, riotous flowers and elegant colonial buildings provide more than just a hint of the tropics.

Beautiful Brisbane glowing by night.

Albert Street — Methodist Church.

City Hall.

Story Bridge.

Queen Street Mall.

The magnificent Surfers Paradise skyline.

TROPICAL NORTH QUEENSLAND

Ellis Beach.

Hinchinbrook Island.

Green Island.

A climate from the heavens!

Rockhampton.

Rosslyn Bay, Yeppoon.

Townsville viewing Castle Hill.

Townsville Plaza.

Sugar cane fields.

NORTHERN TERRITORY

Australia's Northern Territory is a vast land of surprising contrasts. History indicates, that its vast stretches of living desert were actually once a beautiful rain forest. Lack of regular rainfall and lack of substance in the soil destroyed the rain forest, however due to the fertility that still exists, a good rainy season will produce a massive ground cover, myriad carpets of colour, created by the multitude of wildflowers.

Dramatic and picturesque physical features of the Kakadu National Park, Katherine Gorge, Ayers Rock and the mighty MacDonnell Ranges also nurture ancient ferns, palms and cycads of an earlier wetter age.

Ayers Rock.

Twin Falls.

Devils Marbles.

The Olgas with Ayers Rock in the background.

Kangaroo.

Koala.

SOME OF AUSTRALIA'S FAVOURITE ANIMALS

Kookaburra.

The windswept, treeless plains of the Nullabor, where water is scarce and tourists hurry across a stretch of a thousand kilometres.

This is the division of the Great South Land.